HOW TO BE A
WAY COOL
GRANDFATHER

D1490498

HOW TO BE A WAY COOL GRANDFATHER

Verne Steen

Photographs by Marlene Hannah

Mustang Publishing Co.
Memphis, TN

Library of Congress Cataloging-in-Publication Data

Steen, Verne, 1927-
    How to be a way cool grandfather / Verne Steen.
       p.   cm.
    ISBN 0-914457-74-8 (pbk. : alk. paper)
    1. Toy making. 2. Recycling (Waste, etc.) I. Title.
TT174.S74 1996
745.592--dc20   95-36986
                                           CIP

10 9 8 7 6 5 4 3 2 1

To my grandchildren

*Brian Steen, Keith Carmona,
Mark Carmona, Jennie Steen,
Erin Steen, Sean Steen,
Clayton Steen, and Alison Steen*

who are the inspiration

Acknowledgments

I first conceived of this book when grandchildren began appearing in my family at an alarming, yet delightful, rate. I realized that I could tell all my old stories (which my children knew quite well, and were lovingly bored with) again to young, enthralled ears.

I also thought that the toys I had once made for my children would be just as much fun for their children, so I made some do-it-yourself toy kits and gave them as gifts on birthdays or holidays. The youngsters were delighted, and their parents, happy to have fond memories triggered by the simple playthings, were able to show their kids how to make the toys special by using their own "secret" modifications.

In discussions with my family, we decided that a book about these homemade toys might be a good idea. I sat down and roughed out the book with many sketches and ideas. And then I promptly procrastinated for nearly ten years. Finally, at the urging of my good wife Shirley and our children (I'll always think of them as "our children"), I rolled up my sleeves and finished the book.

The book has been read and edited by my entire family. Judy Carmona, our oldest and most enthusiastic, is certain that no one will be able to resist its temptations. If I could only convince the publisher to put her in charge of marketing, she would motivate sales with unflagging energy. Steven Steen, our oldest son and a do-it-yourselfer, has given his time and effort in recalling toy ideas and constructing some of the items, most notably the stilts. Brad Steen, our youngest child and most accomplished toy-maker, remembered toys that I had long forgotten. He was amazed that I could forget about items that he felt were so important to his youth. Shirley, of course, has suffered with my enthusiasm as well as my lethargy and kept me plugging away. Their reward will be a copy of the book and my heartfelt thanks and love.

Photographer Marlene Hannah was a lifesaver. I owe much to her efforts to make the photos more artistic when I was too focused on description. And I'm grateful to all the youngsters who agreed to be models in the photos: Tyler, Elliott, and Ryan George, Rebecca Baer, Henry Rothenberg, and my grandchildren Sean, Alison, and Jennie Steen.

Publisher Rollin Riggs has been helpful, friendly, and communicative. He has made my first voyage into writing an enjoyable experience.

Everyone with whom I have shared my ambition to produce this book has been supportive, and many reminded me of their favorite toys. But most of all, my thanks go to my grandchildren. Without the inspiration they give by simply being themselves, I could never have finished this project. With their enthusiasm, interest, excitement, and joy—all reminiscent of my youth—they've made the chore of creating this book worthwhile. They allow me to recapture adventures I'd long forgotten—and they make them all the more pleasurable by letting me see through their eyes.

Verne Steen

Contents

Acknowledgments   vii

Introduction   xv

Pea Shooter   3

Straw Tooter   7

Willow Whip Arrow-Thrower   10

Rubber Slingshot   13

Rubber Band Gun   18

Leather Sling	22
Toothpick Springer	25
Figure Four Trap	27
Kite	30
Kite Parachute	34
Helicopter Propeller	37
Helicopter Propeller (with String)	40
Stilts	43
"Two Little Blackbirds..."	47
Mystery Propeller	50
Bullroarer	53
Button Spinner	56
Mystery Latch	58
Dart	62
Spool Crawler	65
Popsicle Stick Trick	68
Rattlesnake Eggs	71
Rubber Band Jumper	74
Coin-in-the-Hair	77
Tin Can Telephone	80

Box Making   83

Paddle Wheel Boat   86

Willow Whistle   90

Bent Paper Match Trick   94

Cootie Catcher   97

Introduction

"Rad, Dad, that's bad!" my 10-year-old grandson exclaimed. "Totally awesome!"

I had just handed him a toy that took me 30 minutes to make. Though I wasn't exactly sure what he had said, I quickly deduced by his enthusiastic attitude that he liked my little gift.

"You are a way cool Grandpa," he said matter-of-factly as he ran outside to play with his new toy.

I had to think about that one. I'd heard "cool" quite a bit from my grandchildren, and I knew it was a term of approval. "Way cool," I decided, must be much better. I've since learned that "way cool" is high praise indeed, and, thanks to my toys, I've been "way cool" for years.

Being Way Cool

If you're old enough to be a grandfather, you might think that being "way cool" is not much of an accomplishment, or worse, undignified. I beg to differ.

First, just being a grandfather isn't much to be proud of. Anyone can be a grandfather quite naturally, provided he has sired the offspring to allow such an event. It's how one treats his offspring that deserves praise or scorn. In my case, I feel a big responsibility to my grandchildren, and I try to teach them the important life lessons that will help them grow up and, someday, become responsible grandparents themselves.

The key word above is "teach." Teaching is hard work. Though your lessons might include many subjects—religion, philosophy, mathematics, etc.—I most enjoy teaching the entertaining, fun things that I learned as a kid. To me, a big part of being a way cool grandfather involves passing on my time-tested knowledge for the enjoyment of this generation.

I seem to have more time and patience than many other adults, so my grandchildren listen to me. (Indeed, they seem to listen to me much better than my children did when they were growing up!) Of course, the fact that I cater to them and don't scold them as much as their parents probably has a lot to do with their attentiveness. Whatever the reasons, I find I have great opportunities to convey things that my grandkids might not otherwise hear and learn.

Not that I think of myself as "The Wise Old Man of the Mountain," imparting rare wisdom to my little disciples. Rather, I know so many things—much of which I learned as a youngster—that are unknown even to my own children! Some of this, like the Cootie Catcher, is pure entertainment, learned in a time before TV and Toys Я Us. And some is fun but more educational, like the leather sling, which demonstrates fundamental laws of physics. (The sling demonstrates centrifugal and centripetal force, and how to control these forces for desired effects.) These toys can provide a basic understanding of nature that I hope my grandchildren will find useful throughout their lives and helpful in grasping more complex ideas.

Now, you might despair that, compared to the latest computer game or music group, you could never compete in the Way Cool Olympics. Well, don't sell your grandchildren short. You'll be surprised at what kids today think is cool. They're very savvy children for the most part, and they usually know the difference between the superficial "advice" of a rock star on MTV and the honest, sincere thoughts of an elder who's willing to take the time to enjoy simple things with them. You might also be surprised to find that they think building fun toys inexpensively is "way cooler" than buying expensive toys that never live up to the hype they see on Saturday morning cartoons. (They're savvy consumers, too.)

Toys Today

One of the problems with toys today, in my opinion, is that they do nearly everything for the child and leave little room for improvisation and imagination. Every activity you can do with a doll or a toy truck has been shown repeatedly on TV—and children can be reluctant to deviate from these scripts. And the toys themselves can be so complicated that a child will never understand how they work. I well remember my fascination with taking broken toys apart to see their innards and figure out why the parts moved as they did. Today, a broken toy is likely to yield a maze of electronic circuitry that would require a Ph.D. to understand! And I always loved to modify my toys to make them "special" or "better." But there's no way to alter many of today's toys, much less repair them. So, one of the great values of the toys in this book is their flexibility. They can be changed, repaired, and tailored to the individual child with little trouble.

The bottom line is this: The toys in this book teach children new skills, make them use their imaginations, and let them spend quality time with a loving adult. Trust me, that is always "way cool."

Making These Toys

You and your grandchildren can make most of the toys described with a few simple tools and materials found around the house or yard. As a child, I always kept a lookout for items like castoff boots, gloves, inner tubes, and such. The boots and gloves were a good source of leather for various projects, and the inner tubes (real rubber in those days—now the tubes are synthetic and not as elastic) were great for making rubber band guns and slingshots.

When making these toys, I've found that kids think it's more fun if they use everyday items found nearby. It teaches them about recycling, and it expands their imaginations when they see, for example, a glove taken apart and transformed into something else. If you must purchase materials, try buying from a leather shop, hobby shop, shoemaker, etc.—all of which will require imagination and careful selection—rather than getting something that comes packaged and pre-measured. You'll find that the youngsters can get very choosy about the materials that go into their toys. Developing their powers of discrimination now will help them in later life when they must select more important items like cars, homes—and spouses.

Though I describe using drills, saws, and other tools to make these toys, a Boy Scout-type pocketknife—with a large blade, a small blade, a screwdriver blade, and an auger blade—should be sufficient to make almost everything. You can drill a decent hole with the auger blade, and, while a saw will make quick work of cutting a board, I have "worried" many pieces in two with a knife. So if your grandchild has a knife and wants to use it, let him or her try, and use the opportunity to discuss knife safety, the properties of the materials, the advantages of various tools, etc.

You can build most of these toys quickly, but time shouldn't be a factor. Remember, the time you spend with your grandchildren on these projects is far more important than the projects themselves—though of course the kids won't realize this until they're older. Plus, you'll be astonished at the speed with which a child can reproduce an item once he's made it and decided it was fun. Then, the youngster will start teaching a friend!

Improving the Toys

Tailoring these toys to your grandchild is almost as important as making them in the first place. If a child is left-handed, for example, be sure to take that into account during construction. Kids often want to put their initials on a piece, so try making a branding iron out of a coat hanger. When heated on a stove, a hanger can let the youngster burn his own special "brand" into the wood—and give you a chance to teach heat- and fire-safety lessons.

Further, you can make numerous improvements to all of these toys. I have kept refinements out of the descriptions on purpose, because children will discover them as they play. Some of the toys, such as the Spool Crawler and the Rattlesnake Eggs, appear clearly (and deliberately) crude in the photos. Encourage your youngsters to notice this and make their versions look better. You'll see their pride when they show you how they improved on the item you built together. (For example: With the toy on page 10, they'll learn that the tip section of Grandpa's old fishing pole is a good substitute for a willow branch. Then they'll see that the fishing pole makes a good launcher for balsa wood glider planes.) This helps them develop confidence in their ability to think independently, so be sure to praise their efforts— even if you think it messes up your toy!

By the way, if you've never been exposed to the joys of making your own toys and playthings, good! You get the double pleasure of learning to make them alongside your grandchildren.

Problems and Cautions

I confess that my arthritis occasionally made building some of these pieces difficult. But most of the construction is so simple and brief that my ailments never stopped me. However, if arthritis and such trouble you, turn the work over to the youngsters. Their young hands will welcome the chore, and they'll be thrilled because not only are they doing the "grown-up" work themselves, they're also helping Grandpa!

Though these toys are fun to make and use, I must note a few words of caution. We made these items when we were kids because "store bought" toys were scarce. We didn't do a safety analysis to discern all the things that could possibly go wrong, nor did we conform to OSHA requirements when we used our tools. So, of course, we cut and injured ourselves in all kinds of ways and with all manner of tools, and we learned some painful lessons about such things.

As a grandfather, you must provide a buffer for your grandchildren and help them have the joy without the pain. In describing the toys, I've tried to point out the potential dangers that I learned the hard way, but I'm sure I've missed many, so use utmost caution building and using these items. It's good, practical sense, as well as a crucial lesson to teach your youngsters.

When you make toys, don't be too much of a stickler for accuracy. I'm certainly not; the dimensions I describe are often preceded by the word "about." So if you think you should make something smaller or larger, feel free to do so. If the child helping you is a little off in measurement, let it go (though the old line, "Measure twice; cut once" is a valuable life lesson). You'll know if accuracy is crucial to the construction. Remember, we made these toys under the crudest of conditions, and they usually worked fine. If they didn't, we figured out why and fixed them. It's also important that the toy fit the youngster. If a change gives it a better "feel" to your grandchild, then change it. In doing so, you make it special. These toys will help youngsters learn that whatever the item, it can be changed to suit their own needs.

Teaching with the Toys

You'll find that your grandchildren will watch and listen to you intently while you make toys with them. At such times, they are highly receptive to simple but important lessons.

When you transform a clothespin into a pea shooter, for example, you have a great opportunity to talk about recycling, thrift, respect for others' safety, etc. In the toys, the youngsters will see the tangible aspects of the lessons, and they will use these fundamental lessons their entire lives. I know I have.

Because the toys are, or can be, created from leftover and discarded materials, they each promote concepts of thrift, initiative, creativity, and recycling. And as they make their own toys, the kids learn independence, individualism, and the satisfaction that comes with achievement.

An example: When you teach the Popsicle Stick Trick, discuss patience and perseverance. When the kids first try it, they'll be clumsy and might get frustrated. But encourage them to practice, and soon their muscle control will improve and they'll see the fun results of their effort.

Another example: When I consider gullibility and trickery, I always think of the Bent Paper Match Trick. Even some adults fall for it. The lesson here: Never bet on another person's game.

If you've ever walked on stilts, you know the feeling of awe at how different things can look from just a foot higher. It's a change in perspective, and you can teach this in both the literal and metaphysical sense. Whenever I build stilts, I'm preparing my young helpers for the moment when they step up to a new height—and see everything in a different way. I always get a comment like, "I see what you mean! Everything's the same, but it's different!"

Another lesson these toys teach is one that *you* will learn. As you make the toys with your young charges, you'll discover how important you are to your grandchildren. They look to you as one who's survived a life that they're just beginning, and they'll expect guidance, patience, and occasionally discipline. Anything you say carries great weight with youngsters, simply because "Grandpa says so."

I've included a line or two with most of the items about lessons and morals you can teach with the toy. My moral tips are simple and hardly exhaustive, so feel free to add concepts that you think are also appropriate. (But be careful not to overdo it—one or two fundamental lessons per toy is all most youngsters can absorb.) Or, you can skip all the preachy stuff and concentrate on just having fun making and playing with the toys. That time together, in and of itself, will be a great experience for your grandchildren.

My Chauvinism

I want to apologize in advance if you think the tone of this book is unfairly weighted toward boys. As my daughter reminds me regularly, I was raised in an era of chauvinism. Nevertheless, she enjoyed making most of these toys when she was a girl (as I recall, she was darn good with a rubber band gun) and now has a great time sharing them with her two boys. She said that reading my manuscript reminded her of all the fun she had making toys with her brothers. Plus, her ability to create toys and use various tools has made her the envy of the other den mothers in the Cub Scouts.

Along these same lines, some might ask why the title isn't *How to Be a Way Cool Grandmother*. Well, though many grandmothers don't have the same experience as men with certain tools, some of the toys might actually be easier for women to make than men, because of their more nimble fingers and experience with delicate objects. Certainly, all of the toys herein can be made by grandmothers as well as grandfathers. But since I'm a grandfather, and since I was raised in a time when girls played with dolls and kitchen items and boys built more action-oriented toys, I decided to leave the title as is and hope that grandmothers will forgive my deep-rooted chauvinism.

Of course, the main ingredient for these toys is the simple desire to have fun and spend time with your grandchildren, and I know grandmothers are just as "way cool" as grandfathers in this regard.

In Conclusion

Don't expect to find any earth-shaking knowledge or priceless moral lessons in this book. It's a simple, straightforward recollection of enjoyable things that are rather unusual today. If you find there's deep wisdom herein, it's only because the deepest wisdom is found in the simplest, most obvious places, where we rarely look.

I hope these toys help you recall some things you made or did as a child and inspire you to pass on your knowledge—not only of toy-making, but also of life. Truly, it's our greatest legacy to our grandchildren.

HOW TO BE A
WAY COOL
GRANDFATHER

Pea Shooter

Ages: 6-15

Materials Needed:

- a one-piece wood clothespin
- a spring-type wood clothespin
- small, dried peas or beans

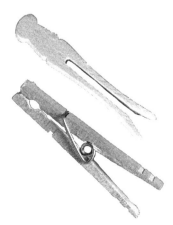

Tools Required:

- pocketknife

Safety Considerations:

Teach your grandchildren never to point the pea shooter at someone's face, as there is a risk of eye injury. Also, be careful about the "ammo" they use in it. Sharp, pointed objects can injure, and small, round objects can get stuck in ears and noses, especially with very young children.

Construction:

Disassemble the spring-type clothespin into its three pieces. Take one of the pieces and notch it (as shown in photos 1 and 2) by squaring off one side of the existing rounded notch where the coiled part of the spring normally rests. Very little wood needs to be removed to square off the notch. Don't make the notch too deep; otherwise, the spring won't come out easily when you pull the trigger. In fact, the wrong end of the spring will come out if the notch is too deep.

Install the metal spring on the notched piece as shown in photo 2. This may take some effort, especially if you have a good, springy spring. If the metal in the spring is soft, the pea shooter will be easy to assemble but won't function as well. It's easiest to start the thin, tapered end of the notched piece into the spring

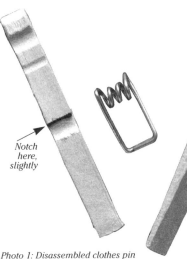

Notch here, slightly

Photo 1: Disassembled clothes pin

first, keeping the coiled part on the side away from the squared-off notch. Then, slide the spring along the notched piece past the squared-off notch until it drops into the notch on the opposite side. Insert the assembled notched piece into the one-piece clothespin as shown in photo 3. Using the remaining wood piece as a "cocker," push the spring back until it catches in the notch. The pea shooter is now cocked.

Load it by inserting a pea or bean in front of the spring piece (see photo 4). When you pull the "trigger," the projectile will shoot several feet.

Children are ingenious at finding clever ways to use things like this, so you must be watchful that they aren't loading it with dangerous items or pointing it at other children's eyes, mouths, etc.

A great source of "ammunition" is mud shaped into small pellets and sun-dried. When the spring strikes this ammo, the mud pellet explodes in a small cloud of dust, resembling the smoke from a gun. It's quite harmless and a great way for kids to play "cops and robbers" without the risk of eye injury.

Photo 2: notched piece with metal spring

Photo 3: assembled pieces

Photo 4: cocking and loading the pea shooter

Lessons for Consideration:

- recycling
- respect for others' safety
- finding entertainment from mundane objects

Straw Tooter

Ages: 4-10

Materials Needed:

- a drinking straw
  (either plastic or waxed paper)

Tools Required:

- pocketknife

Safety Considerations:

Always use extreme caution when working with a knife around children. Take the time to teach them the safe use of knives.

Construction:

This noisemaker, easy to make at any fast-food restaurant, can be a delight for both grandfather and youngsters—but their parents probably won't receive it with much enthusiasm. Way cool grandfathers are more patient with such things and thus more tolerant when they see the kids having a good time. The best part (or worst, depending on your point of view) is that children can quickly make the toy themselves once they learn the initial construction.

Lay the straw on a flat surface and use a pocketknife to flatten one end and make a sharp crease an inch or so from the tip. (You may need to apply a lot of pressure to flatten a plastic straw.) Then, cut the tip to a point on the flattened end (see photo). Place the cut end in your mouth and blow smoothly. You may need to blow fairly hard if the gap between the two "reeds" is large. The sound will be similar to a "raspberry." Be sure that your lips don't touch the end of the straw, since that will deaden the sound.

The straw tooter

Though plastic straws can be hard to crease, the crease holds and the tooter will last quite a while. Wax paper straws are easy to crease but soon become soggy and unusable. Try both and teach your grandchildren a little lesson about the durability of materials.

While this is just a simple noisemaker, kids love it. It gives them something to do while waiting for their food to arrive, and it teaches. All reed instruments—clarinets, saxophones, oboes, etc.—employ the same principle that produces the noise in the tooter.

The reed instrument was one of the earliest musical devices created. Flute-like items are depicted on cave walls that predate written history. Most people think reed instruments make very pleasant sounds (though I don't think anyone would describe the sound of the tooter as "pleasant"). You may be old enough to know some of the great music of the Big Band era—Dorsey, Goodman, etc.—which featured reed music extensively. The tooter gives you a great chance to expose your grandchildren to this "ancient" music, and you might be pleasantly surprised by their reaction to it!

Lessons for Consideration:

- recycling
- respect for others' peace and quiet

Willow Whip
Arrow-Thrower

Ages: 10-15

Materials Needed:

- a three- or four-foot length of willow branch about half an inch in diameter. Choose one that's as springy as a fishing pole.

- a package of straight-grained cedar shingle shims. You can find them at any building supply store.

- about a foot of string

Tools Required:

- pocketknife
- pruning shears (optional)

Safety Considerations:

Use great caution when working with a knife and make sure the youngsters know knife safety before working on this project. Also, you must teach them how to shoot an arrow safely. The child should know where the arrow's going and what it will hit. You'll need plenty of room to practice shooting arrows with them.

Construction:

Cut the willow branch from a tree with pocketknife or shears. Tie the string to the small end of the branch, and make a non-slipping loop about an inch in diameter six inches down the string. (This is a good time to teach your grandchildren to tie a bowline knot. If you can't tie a bowline, any knot that won't slip will work fine.)

Split about an inch or so of the shingle off and carve the piece to look like the arrow in the photo. (Note: Shingles are thicker at one end—called the "butt end"—and thinner at the other.) Use the butt end of the shingle to make the thick end of the arrow. This makes the thin end of the arrow wide and light, much as feathers on a real arrow would be, and the thick end heavy, providing stability.

Loop the string on the notch at the thick end of the arrow and hold the thin end in one hand and the willow whip in the other. Then bend the whip and release the arrow.

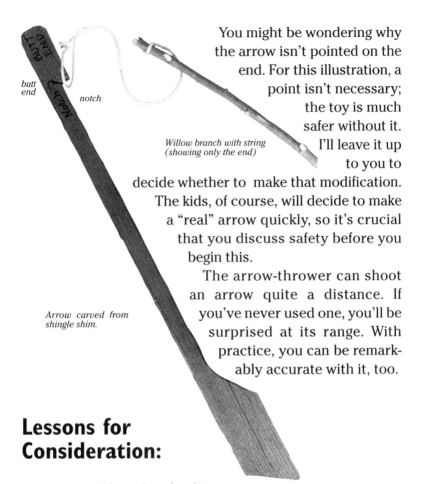

butt end

notch

Willow branch with string
(showing only the end)

Arrow carved from shingle shim.

You might be wondering why the arrow isn't pointed on the end. For this illustration, a point isn't necessary; the toy is much safer without it. I'll leave it up to you to decide whether to make that modification. The kids, of course, will decide to make a "real" arrow quickly, so it's crucial that you discuss safety before you begin this.

The arrow-thrower can shoot an arrow quite a distance. If you've never used one, you'll be surprised at its range. With practice, you can be remarkably accurate with it, too.

Lessons for Consideration:

• respect for others' safety
• respect for others' property

Rubber Slingshot

Ages: 10-15

Materials Needed:

- two ⅜" x 7" rubber bands. (You may want to buy a box of these, since you'll use them for the next toy, too.)
- forked branch of tree or bush
- kite string
- small piece of leather. The tongue of an old shoe or part of an old work glove is ideal.

Tools Required:

- pocketknife
- pruning shears (optional)
- sandpaper

Safety Considerations:

This toy can shoot pebbles, buckshot, marbles, etc. at any target chosen by the shooter. It's very important to teach children what are appropriate targets. Indiscriminate use will always result in an accident—and often an injury.

Construction:

This toy is more complex than most and will stimulate the inventiveness of the builders. There are almost as many variations to this device as there are youngsters who make them. However, I'll describe just the basic model, using materials that kids are likely to find on their own. You'll need to buy rubber bands, though. We used to cut them from old inner tubes, but inner tubes are no longer made of real rubber, and the synthetic rubber isn't elastic enough to work well.

First, find a tree or bush with forked branches. You can make finding the perfect fork a big part of the fun of this project. Though I've seen forks cut from planks or plywood, they always appear bulky and awkward. There is something special about a tree fork that can't be duplicated.

The fork should spread 3-4"wide, and its diameter should be about ½" when peeled (see photo 1). If it's too

Photo 1:
Tree fork
for
slingshot

thin it will break, and if it's too thick it will be hard to use.

Cut the fork from the tree with a pocketknife or shears, and, depending on the tree, peel the bark away while the wood is still wet. (Bark can be hard to remove after the wood has dried.) On a willow tree, for example, the bark will become flimsy and cause the rubber bands to loosen. But some tree bark, such as mesquite and walnut, stays on tight and gives the fork a lovely appearance. Here's a great opportunity for a nature lesson with your grandchildren, so go out to the woods and talk about the various trees and their properties.

At each fork tip, cut a groove about 1/16" deep all around. This provides an indentation for the string that will hold the rubber bands in place (see photo 2). Sand the fork tips to eliminate any sharp edges that could cut the rubber.

groove

Photo 2:
Fork—Peeled,
notched, and
1 rubber band
added

Pocket—
Slit for rubber band

Cut the rubber bands so they are about a foot long. Then, holding one end about 1/2" below the grooved end of the fork, stretch the rubber up and over the other side of the fork. Have a grandchild wrap the string three or four times around the rubber and fork so that the rubber is secure in the groove. Tie the string tightly while the rubber is stretched. When the string is secure and the rubber is released, the rubber will exert pressure on the string to hold it tight. (An alternative to string is a small rubber band. It has the advantage of not needing to be tied, and the disadvantage of being nicked easily and breaking.) Double-check that the rubber band is secure, because if it comes loose from the fork while it's being used it can snap the user in the face.

The next step is to prepare the pocket, which works best when it's pliable and not too thick (about 1" x 2½"). An old leather shoe tongue is ideal; a used leather work glove will work well, too. If there's a rancher's supply store nearby, you can probably find a bundle of thongs, patches, and ties used to repair saddles, harnesses, etc. for a few dollars.

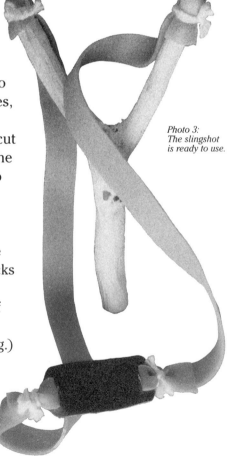

Photo 3:
The slingshot is ready to use.

With a pocketknife, cut a ½" slit at each end of the leather piece (see photo 2). The slits should be about ¼" in from the edges. Thread a rubber band through one of the slits so that ½" or so sticks through. (We always turned the rough side of the leather to grip the stones we were shooting.) Fold it back on itself, pinch it together, stretch it, have someone wrap four or five turns of string tightly around it, and tie it tightly. Thread the other rubber band through the other slit, measure so that the finished rubber bands will be the same length, and tie it the same as the first.

The slingshot is now ready to use.

Of course, a slingshot is a serious weapon as well as a fun toy. My brother-in-law loves to reminisce about growing up as a teenager in the Midwest during the Depression. His family struggled to stay fed and clothed, and he was expected to do his part. Since rifle ammunition was costly, he became quite expert at hunting with a slingshot and provided many rabbits and other small game for the family dinner table. He still retains a fondness for the device.

Though I never hunted with a slingshot, I remember being constantly on the lookout for good "ammo" like ball bearings, marbles, round stones, etc. Of course, I had to think twice before using a marble, because I loved to play marbles, too. And ball bearings were prized by marble players and sort of "illegal" because they were so deadly in the game. So, I usually shot only the smallest of the ball bearings, since they weren't much good for marbles.

Lessons for Consideration:

- respect for others' safety
- respect for others' property
- respect for the life of animals

Rubber Band Gun

Ages: 8-15

Materials Required:

- 18" length of 1" x 2" wood (smooth)
- 2" length of 1" x 2" wood (smooth)
- box of ⅝" x 7" rubber bands
- 2 #8 x 2" flat head wood screws
- 2 #4 x ⅝" flat head wood screws
- 1 spring-type clothespin

Tools Required:

- drill motor with wood bits to drill for #4 and #8 wood screws
- screwdriver (Phillips head or flat, depending on type of screw selected)
- sandpaper

Safety Concerns:

Before working with any motorized tool, be sure to give a lesson in tool safety. Plus, this toy can propel a rubber band 10-15 feet, and at close range the rubber band will sting if it hits bare skin—and could injure someone's eye. Make sure the kids understand the potential danger involved with this toy.

Construction:

Attach the two-inch piece of wood to the 18" piece with the two-inch wood screws, as shown in photo 1. Sink the heads of the screws below the surface of the wood to let the rubber bands pass over them freely.

Using the #4 x ⅝" wood screws, attach the clothespin to the two-inch handle about half an inch below the top of the barrel (see photo 2).

Next, test the elasticity of the rubber bands to establish how long to make the "barrel." Though you'll probably get snapped by the rubber band a

Photo 1: Screw on attachment for handle

few times, it's the most expedient way to determine the barrel's proper length.

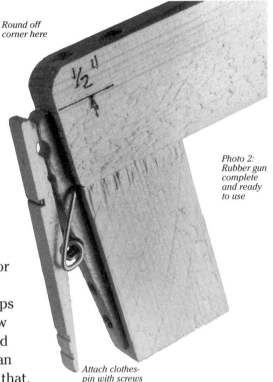

Round off corner here

½ "

Photo 2: Rubber gun complete and ready to use

Attach clothespin with screws

Put one end of the rubber band into the clothespin, then pull it over the top of the gun until you can hook it over the end of the barrel or it slips out of the clothespin. If it slips out, figure out how far it stretched and cut the barrel off an inch shorter than that.

Use the sandpaper to smooth all sharp edges and round off the edge that the rubber band passes over just after it leaves the clothespin. Sharp edges at such places will cut the rubber.

To load a rubber band on the gun, insert it into the clothespin first and then stretch it over the end of the barrel. Take care not to depress the clothespin during loading or you'll get snapped by the rubber band.

Of all the toys my children and grandchildren used, they remember the rubber guns best. They spent countless hours playing with them, and as long as they didn't aim at someone's head, the worst damage was the sting of being "shot" by a rubber band. The sting is sharp enough to startle but never causes any injury (except to pride occasionally).

Nevertheless, you need to remind your grandchildren of the dangers of aiming anything at anyone's face and eyes. Though it's unlikely that a rubber band could cause real damage, getting snapped in the face hurts and ends the fun quickly.

We also developed a rubber band rifle. Since it's longer and stretches the rubber tauter, it packs a noticeably smarter sting. We even created a repeating rifle that was most effective. Once the youngsters get into making their own toys, you'll be amazed at the modifications they devise.

Lessons for Consideration:

- respect for others' safety

Leather Sling

Ages: 10-15

Materials Required:

- piece of leather 1½" x 3" (e.g. a tongue from an old boot)
- two leather strips about ¼" x 18".
  (These might be hard to find, but a leather craft store should have them.)

Tools Required:

- pocketknife

Safety Considerations:

Though the design of this device is old and familiar (remember David and Goliath?), you'll need a lot of practice to use it properly. Projectiles can and will go in the wrong direction, so be sure your grandchildren aren't hurling dangerous objects and are well away from windows and other breakable things. With practice, you can be quite accurate with a sling and throw pebbles and such many yards.

Construction:

Cut the 1½" x 3" piece of leather pocket as shown in the photo. Cut the slits about ⅜" long and about ⅜" from each end of the pocket. Next, cut slits in the two strips at one end. Cut the slits in the center of the strip about ½" long and about ¼" from the end of the strip.

Pass the slit end of one of the strips through the slit in the pocket until about an inch protrudes. Then, take the other end of the strip and pass it through the slit in the strip. Pull all of the strip through until it tightens on the pocket, then pull it snug. Repeat for the other strip.

On the free end of one of the strips, cut a finger slit. The sling is ready to use. Making it is easy; using it well is tough.

End slit for finger

Pocket with ⅜" slits cut at each end

Place the index finger of your throwing hand through the finger slit. Hold the unslit strip between the thumb and middle finger of your throwing hand. Stretch the strips so that the pocket forms a cradle of equal lengths on both sides and hangs down vertically. Place a small stone, marble, etc. in the pocket.

Point your free arm at the target. Carefully swing the sling in an arc halfway between horizontal and vertical until it reaches a point directly overhead, then whip it in a horizontal arc and release the end of the strip in the direction you're pointing. You must keep the sling moving in a smooth motion because centrifugal force keeps the stone in the pocket. If the motion is jerky, the stone will fall out of the pocket and fly somewhere other than the target. Further, if you don't release the strip properly, the sling will whip around you—which can really smart.

When you're teaching your grandchildren how to use the sling, tell them to throw for accuracy at nearby targets first rather than going for distance. As they become more comfortable with the feel of the device, they'll naturally try to increase the distance.

Lessons for Consideration:

- respect for others' safety
- respect for others' property

Toothpick Springer

Ages: 6-15

Materials Needed:

- five flat toothpicks
- matches

Tools Required:

- none

Safety Concerns:

Since fire is involved with this device, be sure to give a stern fire lecture before you begin. The device will scatter burning toothpick pieces over two or three feet, so be sure nothing flammable is nearby. It's also a good idea to have a fire extinguisher handy.

Construction:

Arrange the five toothpicks in the configuration shown in the photo. Set one corner of the array on fire with the match. When the fire burns through any joint, the entire array will spring apart.

This is a very simple device—and its very simplicity makes it a good teaching aid. It demonstrates quite graphically the relief of locked-in stresses when they are suddenly released. The fire shows the danger that can result from such release.

As long as the toothpicks are left alone, they appear harmless and safe. But as soon as some outside force releases them, they can be dangerous.

Lessons for Consideration:

- respect for fire
- elementary lessons of physics and engineering

Figure Four Trap

Ages: 10-15

Materials Needed:

- three ⅜" x ⅜" sticks about 8" long
- box (cardboard, wood, or plastic) about 18" x 18" x 24"

Tools Required

- pocketknife

Safety Concerns:

The Figure Four Trap is simply a box propped up by a trigger mechanism that lets the box trap whatever trips the trigger. Usually, the bait determines what's trapped. If your bait is birdseed, you can't expect to trap a snake. But, be advised that you will trap whatever takes a fancy to the bait—the neighbor's cat, for example. Plus, the trapped creature will probably be scared and resentful, so use caution when looking to see what's caught. You may want to provide a way to see into the box without lifting it up first.

Also, be careful when propping the box on the trigger. If it falls unexpectedly, it will pinch fingers.

Construction:

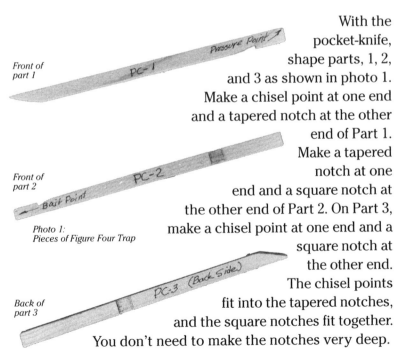

Photo 1:
Pieces of Figure Four Trap

With the pocket-knife, shape parts, 1, 2, and 3 as shown in photo 1. Make a chisel point at one end and a tapered notch at the other end of Part 1. Make a tapered notch at one end and a square notch at the other end of Part 2. On Part 3, make a chisel point at one end and a square notch at the other end. The chisel points fit into the tapered notches, and the square notches fit together. You don't need to make the notches very deep.

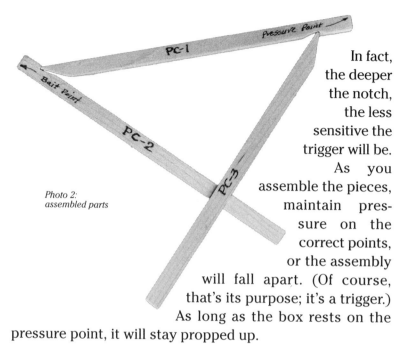

Photo 2:
assembled parts

In fact, the deeper the notch, the less sensitive the trigger will be. As you assemble the pieces, maintain pressure on the correct points, or the assembly will fall apart. (Of course, that's its purpose; it's a trigger.) As long as the box rests on the pressure point, it will stay propped up.

Tie the bait to the bait point and turn it under the box. When something pulls down the bait, the propping sticks will disengage and the trigger will let the box fall to the ground, trapping whatever pulled at the bait. You can make the bait point more sensitive by making it longer from the notch near the end. To adjust the trigger's sensitivity further, you can vary the depth of the notches.

Remember, whatever is trapped will try to escape, so the box must be heavy and strong enough to contain the prey. If it's too light, put some rocks on top to weigh it down.

This simple mechanism can keep youngsters busy all day trying to set it and catch something. Of course, when they do catch something, they have an entirely new set of problems—and so do you! You'll have ample opportunity to discuss two concepts: patience (while waiting to catch something) and kindness to animals (after your patience has been rewarded).

Kite

Ages: 6-15

Materials Needed:

- two or three sheets of newspaper
- a ball of kite string
- half a cup of flour (or white glue)
- two sticks: one ⅛" x ⅜" x 30" long and one 20" long
- four or five 1½" wide strips of rags 18"-24" long

Tools:

- small dish for mixing flour and water
- coping saw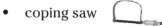
- scissors
- pocketknife

Safety Concerns:

Careful use of the scissors and knife are a must. If the young-sters haven't already been instructed on their proper use, be sure to do so before you begin. Also, you'll need to discuss the safety of kite-flying. None of the materials used in this kite is dangerous, but some people like to use other materials that are. *Never* use wire to make a kite! Wire, kite-flying, and power lines can be a fatal combination. Regardless of the materials, avoid power lines anyway. Find an open field, beach, large park, or similar area.

Construction:

Using the coping saw, make a shallow (about $\frac{1}{16}$" deep) cut in each end of the sticks in the middle of the $\frac{1}{8}$" dimension and parallel to the $\frac{3}{8}$" dimension. Measure from one end of the 30" stick down about nine inches and place the 20" stick there. Fasten the two together with string (see photo 1).

Pass a length of string around the ends of the sticks through the shallow cuts made with the coping saw. The framework for the kite is now complete.

Lay out the newspaper, place the framework on it, and mark a line on it about an inch beyond the string at all points. With scissors, cut the newspaper along the line. Cut a "V" in the newspaper at each of the four corners of the kite frame. (See photo 2.)

With the kite frame on the newspaper, fold over the inch or so of excess paper and crease the paper at the string. Mix some water with flour to make glue, and smear it with your fingers (kids love this part) under the creased edges to glue it to the other side. Let it stand until dry. (This may take some time, so if you're in a hurry, use white glue. While this facilitates the kite's construction, it takes a lot of the fun away from the youngsters.)

Photo 1

9" to top

When the glue is dry, cut about six feet of string and make a yoke for the kite. The yoke gives the kite the proper attitude to the wind, and, in my experience, it's different for each kite. On the paper side of the kite (which faces the wind), fasten one end of the yoke to the sticks where the two sticks are tied together and the other to the bottom of the kite. (A notch in the stick will keep it from slipping.) You'll need to pierce the newspaper at these points. Lay the kite on the floor, gather the string so that it's coming from the cross stick perpendicular to the floor, and tie an overhand knot in the two strings about 18" from the kite. This will leave a loop on which to tie the kite string. Tie the end of the ball of string to the end of the yoke.

Tie one of the rag strips to the bottom of the kite to form a

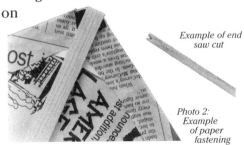

Example of end saw cut

Photo 2: Example of paper fastening

tail, and give the kite a test flight. If it dives and loops, or if the wind is especially strong, you'll need to put a longer tail on the kite. Sometimes, kites fly better without a tail. You'll just have to experiment.

Photo 3: The kite completed

If there's plenty of wind and the kite won't rise up when pulled, try adjusting the yoke so the kite is "flatter" to the wind. Here again, you'll need to experiment. Children thrive on such experiments and adjustments, so be sure to consult them with each modification. They'll learn problem-solving behavior that will help them their entire lives.

Lessons for Consideration:

- thrift
- outdoor safety
- recycling

Kite Parachute

Ages: 6-15

Materials Needed:

- square paper napkin
- straight pin with head
- six feet of thread
- small, weighted objects: a small nut, a bolt or screw, a toy soldier, etc. (shouldn't weigh more than about 2 oz.)

Tools Required:

- pliers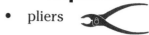

Safety Concerns:

In addition to the concerns expressed in the previous chapter, you should be careful to use the parachute in a very open, flat area. Kids can get so involved in chasing the floating object as it falls from the kite that they forget to watch where they're running.

Construction:

First, fold the napkin or piece of paper in half and then in half again. The fold will mark the location of the center of the square.

Next, fold the thread in half and then half again. This will give four lengths, each about 18" long. Cut the threads at the folds. Tie one thread to each corner of the napkin. Gather the free ends and tie each end of the lengths of thread to the weighted object. Be sure the threads are equal in length.

Take the pliers and make a smooth hook at the sharp end of the pin. The hook should not be parallel to the shank of the pin but should make an angle with it (see photo). Carefully thread the bent pin through the center of the napkin from the inside of the parachute out. When you're holding the pin, only the head of the pin should hold the parachute without tearing through. Gently hook the pin on the string holding the kite and slide the pin as high up the string as possible. Let out some of the kite string, and the wind will take the parachute right up to the kite.

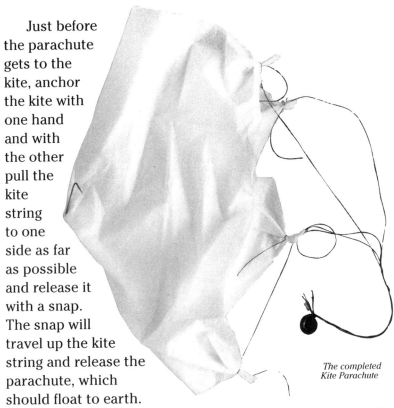

Just before the parachute gets to the kite, anchor the kite with one hand and with the other pull the kite string to one side as far as possible and release it with a snap. The snap will travel up the kite string and release the parachute, which should float to earth.

The completed Kite Parachute

The parachutes can often be used repeatedly, and they'll provide hours of entertainment once plain old kites have lost their allure.

Lessons for Consideration:

- outdoor safety
- elementary understanding of remote controls

Helicopter Propeller

Ages: 10-15

Materials Needed:

- ½" x ⁵⁄₁₆" x 7" piece of soft wood
- a round popsicle stick 7" long (or ³⁄₁₆" dowel)
- white glue

Tools Required:

- pocketknife
- drill motor with drill bit
  the size of popsicle stick or dowel

Safety Concerns:

Be sure to teach proper handling of knives and drills before beginning this toy.

Construction:

Measure 3½" from the ends of the piece of wood and drill the hole for the dowel or popsicle stick. Then, measure 3⅜" from each end of the piece of wood. (Precise dimensions are important to the finished propeller. If you're not careful, the propeller will be unbalanced and wobbly.) The ¾" left in the middle of the piece is the "hub" and will not be carved to make the propeller. It should be marked on all four sides. Next, use the pocketknife to carve away the wood until about ¹⁄₁₆" of wood is left for

The completed propeller

the propeller (see photo). Notice that the material carved away is not the same on each side of the "hub."

Insert the dowel or popsicle stick into the drilled hole. If the hole is a little bit smaller than the stick (about $\frac{1}{64}$"), you'll have to hammer it in. (But it won't need glue, and, since youngsters are often impatient and don't want to wait for glue to set, this can be a good thing.)

Once the stick is in place, hold it between the palms of your hands with the propeller aimed up. Slide your hands in opposite directions rapidly while pressing them together, then release quickly. The action will spin the propeller either up or down. To reverse the direction of the propeller, simply rub your hands the opposite way.

If you aren't satisfied with the propeller's lift, try starting with a stick $\frac{1}{2}$" x $\frac{1}{4}$" x 7". This will reduce the pitch. (A stick $\frac{1}{2}$" x $\frac{3}{8}$" x 7" will increase the pitch.) Such experiments in weight and thickness are great for teaching simple concepts of aerodynamics.

Lessons for Consideration:

- thrift
- simple aerodynamics

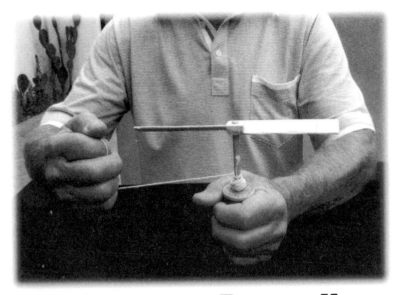

Helicopter Propeller with String

Ages: 10-15

Materials Needed:

- ½" x ⁵⁄₁₆" x 7" piece of soft wood
- a round popsicle stick 7" long (or ³⁄₁₆" dowel)
- white glue
- spool from spool of thread
- three feet of string

Tools Required:

- pocketknife

- drill motor with drill bit
  the size of popsicle stick or dowel

Safety Concerns:

Be sure to teach proper handling of knives and drills before beginning this toy.

Construction:

Using the propeller we made on pages 37–39, wind some string around the propeller shaft near the blade, leaving 8" to 10" of string to wrap around your hand or fingers. Slide the propeller shaft into the thread spool to where the string is wrapped. Hold the spool in one hand and aim the propeller up. Pull the string briskly with the other hand. If the propeller doesn't rise, rewind the string in the opposite direction and try again.

The propeller will rise higher and faster with a spool than with your hands.

If you can't find a thread spool, drill a hole in a piece of dowel or a block of wood for the same effect.

Lessons for Consideration:

- thrift
- mechanical advantages

Stilts

Ages: 8-15

Materials Needed:

- two 5' lengths of 1½" dowel (for the legs)
- about 16" of metal plumber's tape
- one 8" length of 2' x 4' wood (for the steps)
- two pieces of scrap 2' x 4' x 6" wood
- eight #8 x 1" wood screws
- two #8 x 2" wood screws
- four #8 x 2" drywall screws

Tools Required:

- drill motor with a 1½" wood bit and drill bit (to pre-drill #8 drywall screw holes)

- screwdriver (Phillips or flat to match wood and drywall screws)

- #8 wood screw drill bit for wood screws

- saw

- tin snips (or metal shears)

Safety Concerns:

Since the tools for this project are a little more complex than just a pocketknife, be sure to instruct your grandchildren on how to use them safely.

You'll also need to show the kids how to use stilts properly. Though they were common toys during my childhood, they're seldom seen these days. These stilts will raise the user just a foot high, but kids invariably want to get as high as they can. So here's where you'll need extra caution, because the dowels used here won't be strong enough to hold higher steps, nor are these designed to carry anyone heavier than 100 pounds.

If you want to make higher stilts, you'll need to use heavier legs, which are harder to use and clumsier. Still, your youngsters may want you to help them. But with the "better" stilts comes risk, and you should make sure they understand this.

Construction:

First, make the stilts' steps. Measure 4" from each end of the 2' x 4' to mark the center of the edge. Measure 3" from the end of the two scrap 2' x 4' pieces to mark the center of their edges. Line up all three pieces on their center lines and screw them together with a 2" drywall screw about 3" to each side of the center line on both sides. The result: three 2 x 4's screwed together on edge with four drywall screws, and all of the edge center lines lined up. (The ends, of course, won't be lined up.)

On the 8" board, measure about ⅝" from each side to find the center of the edge on the center line. All this preparation will let you drill a 1½" hole across the 3½" width of the 8" board. Such a hole will cut the board in half, making two steps and leaving a curved surface to fit against the 1½" dowel leg. We'll call the drilled edge the "inside edge." Proceed to drill the 1½" hole and part the board.

You might ask, "Why use dowel for the legs? Why not use square cut material and eliminate the effort of drilling the 1½" hole described above?" Simple. The dowel is much easier for a youngster to hold, and it will reduce the risk of splinters.

After parting the steps, remove the drywall screws and discard the scrap boards. Measure 2" from the outside edges (opposite from the inside edges) and cut a 45° angle to remove the corners. Both steps are now complete and ready to be installed.

Measure 12" (or less if a shorter stilt is desired) from one end of the 1½" leg and place the top of the step there with the 45° angle cut facing toward the short end of the leg. Measure the needed amount of plumber's tape and cut it with the tin snips. Cut the sharp corners from the ends to reduce the risk of snags and cuts. Wrap one piece of the metal plumber's tape around the leg and about ¼" down from the top of the step. Fasten it to the leg with one of the #8 x 2" wood screws. Then fasten it to the step with two wood screws on each side of the step. Wrap another piece of metal plumber's tape

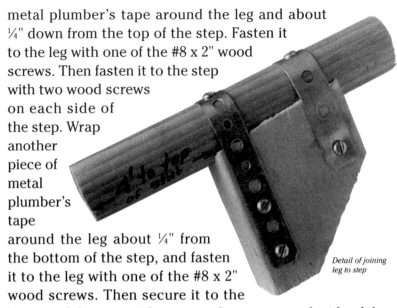

Detail of joining leg to step

around the leg about ¼" from the bottom of the step, and fasten it to the leg with one of the #8 x 2" wood screws. Then secure it to the bottom of the step with one wood screw on each side of the step. Repeat for the other leg.

The stilts are now finished. Round off sharp corners and sand smooth, and be sure to take time to show the youngsters how to use them safely. Remember that they're designed for kids, not adults, and they won't support a weight over 100 pounds.

Lessons for Consideration:

- perspective
- patience with detail

"Two Little Blackbirds..."

Ages: 4-10

Material Needed:

- napkin, tissue, or similar thin paper

Tools Required:

- none

Safety Concerns:

None.

Construction:

Once I was at a dinner party in which the host let his young son join the socializing before dinner. The child, alone among adults, was demanding everyone's attention and generally making a nuisance of himself. When I showed him this trick, he was enthralled and spent the rest of the evening practicing—and leaving the adults alone.

This simple parlor trick never fails to capture the attention of a young audience. I find that, instead of showing how the trick is done, it's better to keep repeating it. The kids will try to copy your actions, and they're usually so intent on succeeding that they never get impatient. And when they do learn the trick, they'll spend hours mastering the moves and showing their friends.

When you have the kids' attention, take the tissue and solemnly tear off two dime-size pieces. Lick each and stick one on each of your index fingers. Place your index fingers on the edge of a table, chair arm, leg of a seated youngster, etc. Curl the rest of your fingers into a fist. Then, recite this poem while you make these moves: "Two little blackbirds sitting on a wall," (raise both hands slightly indicating that the fingers represent the birds); "One named Peter," (raise and drop one hand); "and one named Paul," (raise and drop the other hand); "Fly away Peter!" (raise the first hand smoothly and quickly past your ear, substituting your index finger with your middle finger and returning to the resting spot; curl your index finger into your fist and out of sight); "Fly away Paul!" (do the same maneuver with the other hand).

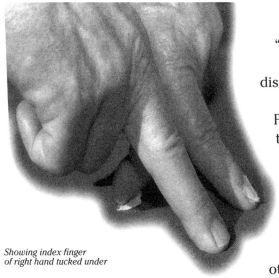

Showing index finger of right hand tucked under

The children will see that the "marked" fingers have magically disappeared! Then, say "Come back Peter!" (reverse the maneuver so that the marked finger is again visible) and "Come back Paul!" (do the same with the other hand). Both marked fingers have returned as if by magic! Without fail, you'll hear gleeful cries of "Do it again!" Repeat until the children want to try it themselves or your patience wears out.

Whether your grandchildren are watching your trick in amazement, or whether they're learning to perform the trick themselves, they'll be thoroughly entertained. And so will you.

Lessons for Consideration:

- trickery
- performing for an audience

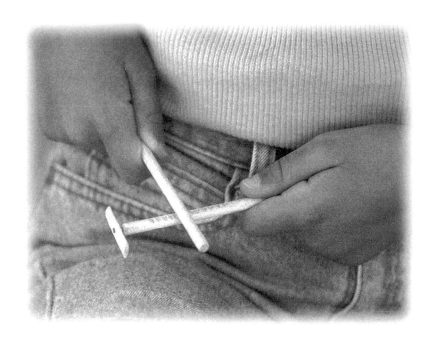

Mystery Propeller

Ages: 6-15

Materials Needed:

- two pieces of ¼" x 6" dowel
- small nail (about ½" long)
- ⅛" x ¼" x 1½" (length) piece of wood

Tools Required:

- pocketknife
- drill with bit a little larger than a nail's diameter
- hammer

Safety Concerns:

Be sure to teach children the proper use of a knife and drill. Because the drill bit is small, it's easy to break, so you'll need extra caution to make sure the drill doesn't slip.

Construction:

Drill a hole in the piece of wood ¾" from each end (i.e., in the middle). The hole should be slightly larger than the nail's diameter to insure the propeller will spin freely. If it doesn't, make the hole a little larger.

Using the pocketknife, cut notches in one of the 6" dowels as shown in the photo. Then, with the nail through the hole in the piece of wood, hammer the nail into the end of the notched dowel nearest the notched end.

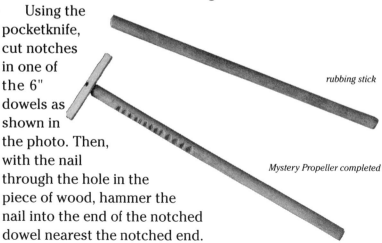

rubbing stick

Mystery Propeller completed

To make the propeller spin, hold the notched dowel horizontally and rub the smooth dowel along the notches. As you rub, if the pressure is on one side of the notches, the propeller will spin one way. If you change the pressure to the opposite side, the propeller will stop and start spinning in the opposite direction. This will mystify youngsters, and they will rub and rub trying to find out how to make it work. Then when they learn, they will want to show their friends.

Lessons for Consideration:

- thrift
- entertainment with mundane objects

Bull-roarer

Ages: 8-15

Materials Needed:

- ⅛" x 2" x 6" piece of Masonite
- piece of cord about six feet long
- fishing line swivel

Tools Required:

- drill with ⅛" bit

Safety Concerns:

Use of the drill is a skill that must be learned. Grandpa is very useful in showing the youngsters how to avoid injury. Be sure to teach good safety practices.

Construction:

Drill a ⅛" hole in one end of the Masonite piece (see photo). Tie a loop in the end of the cord to fit over your wrist, then tie the other end securely to the swivel. Attach the swivel 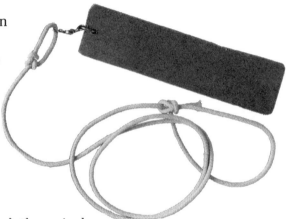 to the Masonite with a piece of string or wire through the hole. To make sound, whirl the bullroarer around your head as fast as you can. The sound will tell you best how to twirl it.

It's possible to change the sound of the bullroarer by making it thinner and narrower. However, this also reduces its weight and makes it harder to twirl. If you drill another hole at the bottom of the Masonite strip, you can add a weight that won't affect the action of the bullroarer. Use another swivel and attach a small lead fishing sinker to it. Or, try a cord that is lighter.

Years ago, men used this device when approaching a battle site as a way to frighten their enemies. So if you think the noise from three children playing with this toy is intolerable, imagine the noise that hundreds of bullroarers would make!

Lessons for Consideration:

- intimidation by noise
- respect for others' peace and quiet

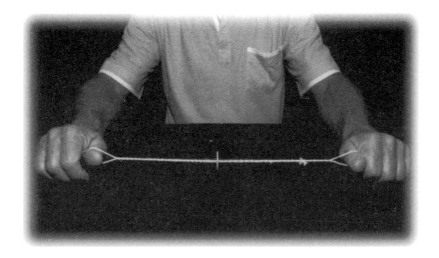

Button Spinner

Ages: 6-15

Materials Needed:

- large button (1" to 1½" in diameter)
- twine small enough to thread through the buttonholes, at least 30" long

Tools Required:

- none

Safety Concerns:

Though this is usually an innocuous toy, it can provide some annoying incidents. If you hold the spinning button against an arm or leg, it will cause a friction burn. If it is placed in one's sister's hair, she and her mother will spend a good bit of time—and some of sister's hair—removing it.

Construction:

Thread the twine through two opposing holes in the button and tie the ends together as shown in the photo. Place your thumbs through the loops on either side of the button. Swing the button with the twine slack so that the button twists the twine. When you pull the twine taut, the button will spin. If you ease off on the tension, the button's inertia will cause the twine to unwind from one direction and wind up the other.

By alternately applying and relaxing tension, the button will spin in one direction and then the other and make a whirring sound. The larger the button, the louder the sound. Also, the more holes in the button, the more sound will be produced.

If you hold the spinning button against a hard surface such as a table top, it will make a buzzing sound that is amplified by the surface. It can, of course, scratch the table top, so watch the children lest they ruin your dining room table.

As a child, I liked to file the button or carve notches in its edges to make more noises.

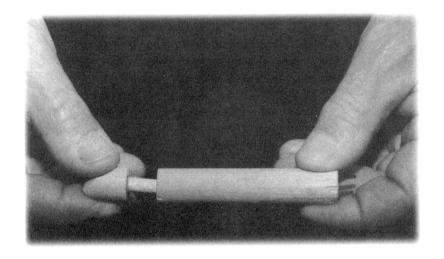

Mystery Latch

Ages: 10-15

Materials Needed:

- 4" length of ⅝" wood dowel
- 3" length of ¼" wood dowel
- white glue
- small rubber band

Tools Required:

- drill motor with ¼" and ⅜" drill bits
- 2 sheets of sandpaper (1 fine, 1 coarse)
- pocketknife
- saw
- rasp or file (optional)

Safety Concerns:

Though this toy is harmless, making it involves tools that can injure those unfamiliar with their use. This toy presents an excellent opportunity to teach safe tool use. For example, drilling the ⅜" hole in the ⅝" dowel is not the easiest thing for a youngster (or anyone) to do. If you're uncomfortable using the dowel, change the design and substitute flat stock, which is easier to clamp and hold. The tube doesn't have to be round; the Latch just looks nicer if it is.

Construction:

The photo for this toy shows five pieces of wood, though the toy consists of only two pieces. The other pieces are intermediate stages in the construction.

First, cut off ¾" of the ⅝" dowel and drill a ¼" hole in one end of it about ⅜" deep. Glue the ¼" x 3" dowel into the hole. Carve a hook into the end of the ¼" dowel.

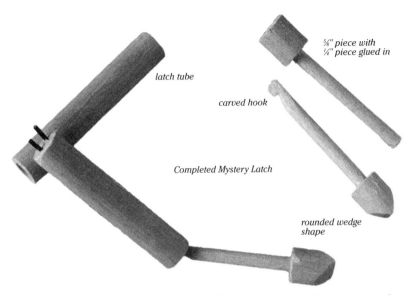

⅝" piece with
¼" piece glued in

latch tube

carved hook

Completed Mystery Latch

rounded wedge
shape

Place the larger dowel on a flat surface and rasp or rub it with the sheet of coarse sandpaper so it has a rounded wedge shape. Smooth it with fine sandpaper. The shape is the most important part of the design, so make it carefully.

Next, drill a ⅜" hole about 3" deep in one end of the ⅝" dowel. Drill a ¼" hole in the other end of the ⅝" dowel until it meets the ⅜" hole.

Cut a piece of ¼" dowel about ⅜" long for a plug, and take a short piece of rubber from the small rubber band. Glue the plug into the end of the dowel with the ¼" hole along with the piece of rubber band so that two ends of the rubber band protrude about ⅜". The rubber loop should not be inside the larger dowel too far beyond the plug. It should be a visible loop (and others will look inside to be sure there is a loop there) in the bottom of the ⅜" hole. But it should be far enough down that it cannot be accidentally hooked.

Hold the tube in one hand and the handle between the thumb and index finger of the other hand, then twist and "feel" until you state, "I've hooked it." When you partly withdraw the handle (never exposing the hook), it looks as though you're pulling against the stretch of the rubber. Then, squeeze the handle with your thumb and index finger until it snaps out of your fingers and back into the tube. It appears that the rubber has snapped it back.

Of course, when others try, they can't "hook" the rubber band. If they ask you to stretch the rubber band out so they can see it, you should express fear that you'll break the rubber band. Very deceptive!

When the youngsters learn the trick, they'll have even more fun using it on their friends as they did watching you. And, of course, they'll know how to make it themselves!

Lessons for Consideration:

- trickery
- gullibility

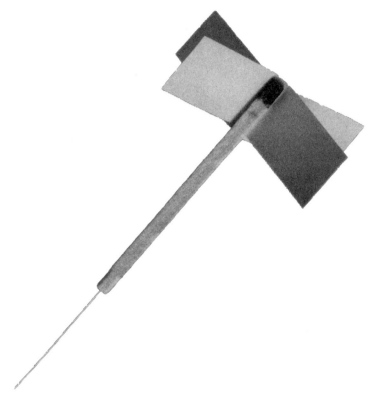

Dart

Ages: 10-15

Materials Needed:

- large wood match
- needle
- paper

Tools Required:

- pocketknife
- pliers

Safety Concerns:

To be frank, darts are dangerous, so you'll need to precede this toy with a stern safety lecture. Use caution pushing the needle into the matchstick, too. If you're not careful, the needle will slip out of the match, or the match will split, and you'll get jabbed in the finger.

Construction:

Strike a match, extinguish it immediately, and clean the carbon off. Using pliers, carefully push a needle into one end of the match about ¼" to ⅜" deep, with the sharp end of the needle pointing out. With a thin-blade knife or razor blade, split the other end of the matchstick about ⅜" from the end.

Next, cut two strips of paper about ⅜" x 1½" long. Slide the strips into the slit end of the matchstick and separate them to form fins. You should have something that resembles the item in the photo.

It's easy to make fun targets for darts. It's also wise: If your grandchildren have specific targets, they're less likely to throw darts at your furniture or each other. If they do get rambunctious, remember that the needle makes such a small mark as to be almost invisible.

Because the dart has four fins, it is much more stable in flight than the arrow of the Willow Whip Arrow-Thrower, which has only one fin. Compare the two with your grandchildren, and let them judge which they prefer.

Lessons for Consideration:

- thrift
- simple aerodynamics
- respect for others' safety

Photo shows opposite ends of the same spool.

Spool Crawler

Ages: 4-10

Materials Needed:

- empty wooden thread spool
- two rubber bands
- two large wood matches (used)
- small washer
- white glue

Tools Required:

- pocketknife

Safety Concerns:

Be sure to review pocketknife safety before making this toy.

Construction:

If you can't find a wooden thread spool, you can use a plastic one, but the spools made of styrofoam probably won't be satisfactory.

First, notch the outer edges of the two flanges of the spool with the knife. The notches will give the Crawler traction when it's dragged over small obstacles.

Next, break off a piece of one of the matches to be shorter than the diameter of the spool. Thread the rubber band through the spool and slip the short matchstick through one end of it. Anchor the matchstick to the spool with a drop of white glue. (See photo 1.)

Over the other end of the rubber band, place the small washer between the matchstick and the spool. (See photo 2.) If the washer has a rough side and a smooth side, place the rough side next to the spool. The washer is important because it greatly reduces

Photo 1

Photo 2

friction and is the key to a mobile Crawler. Slide a long matchstick over the washer and through the end of the rubber band.

Hold the spool in one hand and wind up the rubber band using the long matchstick. Place the assembly on the floor and watch it scoot off as the rubber band unwinds.

A simple little item that provides hours of fun, this toy will crawl over most small obstacles. In fact, if you build a stairway of magazines or something similar, it will crawl up the steps. It can be used in a sandbox or on the ground and is very durable (and easy to fix if it breaks).

Lessons for Consideration:

- thrift
- recycling

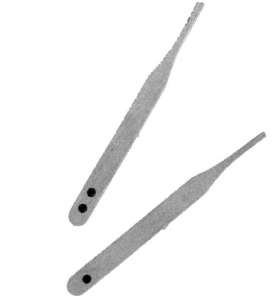

Popsicle Stick Trick

Ages: 6-15

Materials Needed:

- popsicle stick

Tools Required:

- pocketknife
- stencil for making a small dot (optional)
- pencil or pen _____.

Safety Concerns:

Be sure to review the safe use of a pocketknife with your grandchildren before making this toy.

Construction:

With the pocketknife, whittle the popsicle stick into the shape shown in the photo. On one side of the stick, mark two dots. On the other side of the same stick, in about the same area, mark one dot. (see photo 2).

Hold the thin end of the "paddle" between your thumb and fore-finger and show the observer the two dots (see photo 1). Then, as you turn your hand over, twirl the paddle so the two dots are still showing (see photo 3). Turn your hand back, twirl the paddle again, and the two dots are still the only mark visible. It appears that both sides are marked with two dots because the observer has never seen the side with one dot. (In photo 2, the camera stopped the action to show the single dot, but if you twirl the paddle correctly, your audience won't see it.) It takes a little practice (but not much) to make the illusion smooth.

Photo 1: position of hand at start of trick

Photo 2: position of hand while twirling the paddle

Now you're ready to make a dot vanish and then reappear. Concoct some silly stories to accompany the trick, and make a few phony paddles— some with a single dot on each side, and some with two dots on each side. Give

Photo 3: position of hand after twirl

these to your audience and encourage them to make the dots appear and disappear. Their failure to mimic your actions will enhance the illusion. Just be careful that they don't inspect your paddle closely!

Youngsters enjoy being fooled. When they know you're going to fool them, they look forward to it and take it as a challenge. When they discover the trick themselves, they feel they've accomplished something, so be sure to praise them for their astuteness. Showing them that some things are not what they seem is a lesson they'll treasure their whole lives.

This simple trick is a great way to teach kids to be aware and cautious, even when their eyes tell them to proceed.

Lessons for Consideration:

- trickery
- gullibility
- performing for an audience

CAUTION!
RATTLESNAKE EGGS

Rattlesnake Eggs

Ages: 6-15

Materials Needed:

- large paper clip
- two rubber bands
- one washer
- envelope

Tools Required:

- needle nose pliers
- pen or pencil

Safety Concerns:

Teach children how to use the pliers so their fingers don't get pinched. It's happened to me on several occasions, and while it's hardly a serious injury, it does smart—and it takes the fun out of making the toy.

Construction:

First, use the pliers to bend the clip to the shape shown in the photo. Then attach the rubber bands to the washer and the paper clip frame. 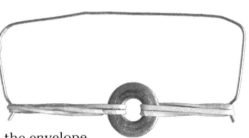 On the envelope, write "RATTLESNAKE EGGS." With the washer, wind up the rubber bands as much as possible without deforming the frame too much. While squeezing the sides so that the washer does not unwind, place the assembly in the envelope.

Make up a story about the mysterious eggs in the envelope, and tell your audience to open the envelope carefully to examine the eggs. When he opens the envelope, the washer will unwind with a startling buzzing sound.

If you wind up this device and put it under your leg while you're seated, it can serve as an alternative to the famous "whoopee cushion." Just raise your leg and let the washer unwind. Since it replicates a certain body function, young-sters find it hilarious and will use it incessantly. Be advised, though, that they're sure to use it to your embarrassment at some point.

Lessons for Consideration:

- trickery
- gullibility

Rubber Band Jumper

Ages: 10-15

Materials Needed:

- rubber bands

Tools Required:

- none

Safety Concerns:

None.

Construction:

Learning to manipulate the rubber band for this trick requires only a modicum of practice. The size of the rubber band is not critical, but it shouldn't be too large or too small. You'll quickly figure out the size that suits you best.

The trick, as seen by the observer, is baffling: A rubber band jumps from around two fingers to two adjacent fingers. This happens in plain view of the observer, who can even watch while you fasten the rubber band onto your fingers.

Photo 1

Here's how it works. Place a rubber band around your index and middle fingers (see photo 1). Next, pull the rubber band out from the palm of your hand so that all four finger tips will be under the band, as in photo 2. Then make your hand into a tight fist.

Photo 2

As seen from the outside of your fist (as in photo 1), the rubber band is clearly around your top two fingers. When you flex your hand and open your fist, it snaps to the bottom two fingers.

With just a little practice, you can place the rubber band smoothly and quickly so that even people observing closely can't figure it out. Children especially love this trick because it's so easy. And once they learn it, they spend hours showing their friends.

Lessons for Consideration:

- trickery
- performing for an audience

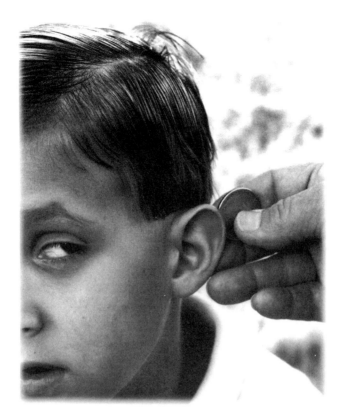

Coin in the Hair

Ages: 6-15

Materials Needed:

- any coin

Tools Required:

- none

Safety Concerns:

None—though occasionally small children are tempted to put the coin in their mouths or noses.

Construction:

Any toy or trick involving money is bound to be a big hit with grandchildren! They are fascinated with it (as are most adults). I always keep loose change in my pocket when I'm around them because it's always useful. At swimming parties, for example, toss a handful of coins in the pool if the kids are getting restless. They'll dive for "treasure" for hours.

Whenever I have the opportunity, I ask children if they need some money. Of course, they always answer yes. So I reach into the child's hair and pull out a coin, which I had palmed, and ask, "Well, why don't you just use the money in your hair?" The younger ones are fooled for a while. As they get older, they know the trick but never admit it because they fear the money will stop! Though it's a simple little trick, my children and grandchildren say they treasure their memories of it.

For this—and most any interaction with your grandchildren—to work, you must understand their perspective. You're the grandfather, so, in their eyes, you have limitless funds and are happy to give your money to them. Fortunately, pulling coins from a child's hair every so often won't cost you much, and you can maintain their illusions. (Of course, as they get older, the illusion is more expensive to maintain!)

An especially good time to use this trick is when you hear the ice cream vendor in the neighborhood. Be sure to have plenty of change (or large coins).

Lessons for Consideration:

- trickery
- value of money

Using the completed phone. (Note: wire shortened for photo.)

Tin Can Telephone

Ages: 10-15

Materials Needed:

- two tin cans (soup cans are ideal)
- 25 feet of bare wire
- epoxy glue (quick-drying type)

Tools Required:

- small nail
- hammer

Safety Concerns:

Since the glue can irritate skin, be sure to follow the safety instructions on the glue package. And double-check to make sure there are no sharp edges anywhere on the cans.

Construction:

The idea behind the tin can telephone is simple: The bottom of the can acts as a diaphragm, which is vibrated by sound coming from a voice. These vibrations are transmitted by the wire to the other can, causing its bottom to vibrate and produce sounds. It's a crude analog to the telephones we use daily.

Choose cans that have a rolled rim at both ends. Some of the newer cans are rolled only at one end, and they won't be as suitable. Also, look for cans that have the concentric ring formations on the ends (as in the photo). This type of can end closely resembles a diaphragm and produces good sound. Though the cans shown in the photo are shorter than standard cans, they worked fine.

I recommend using wire for the best effect, but you could also use heavy thread or kite string. If you use string, make sure it's tightly attached to the can.

Clean the cans and completely remove the top from one end with a can opener. On the other end, use the nail to punch two small holes in the middle. The hole should be only large enough for the wire to be threaded through it. Pass about ½" of wire through the hole on one can, bend it over, then pass it through the other hole. Twist the wire together for a tight fit, and anchor it in place with a big drop of epoxy glue. Do the same thing to the other end of the wire.

The connection of the wire to the can is critical. Be sure that the glue has time to set and that it's dry and hard before you try to use the telephone. If you can solder or weld the wire, the toy will work even better.

Find a space where the wire can be stretched straight and taut for its full length. Gently stretch the wire tight and speak into one of the cans. On the other end, the person should hold the can to his ear. The sound will be somewhat distorted but should be understandable.

Usually, a controversy will develop: Is the wire actually carrying the sound, or would you hear the other person's voice anyway? In truth, it's a little bit of both. The important thing is that the youngsters are experimenting with actual physical phenomena and profiting to the extent that they can ask those very questions. Encourage them to devise controls on the device so they can prove what's really happening.

Lessons for Consideration:

- recycling
- simple physics of vibrations and sound

Box Making

Ages: 6-15

Materials Needed:

- an 8" square and an 8⅛" square of cardboard (the back of a tablet is ideal)
- paper (holiday cards, foil paper, card stock, construction paper, poster board, special paper glued to card stock)
- white glue

Tools Required:

- scissors
- pencil 
- ruler

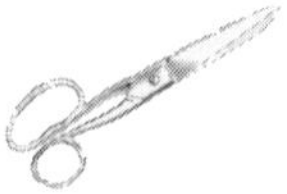

Safety Concerns:

Though scissors are a common item, they can be danger-ous, so be sure to give a safety lecture before you proceed. Very young children should use only blunt-nosed scissors.

Construction:

To begin, select the type of paper for the box. If it's your first box, start with plain, heavy paper. This way, you'll make your mistakes on inexpensive materials.

Use the 8" square of cardboard as a template to cut the box paper to the correct size for the box bottom. The 8⅛" tem-plate is for the box top. Both top and bottom are constructed the same way. For this illustration, we've used a 4" square. (Construction of a box is not dependent on its size.) A 4" square produces a box about 1½" x 1½" x ¾"; an 8" square produces a box about 3" x 3" x 1½"; and so on.

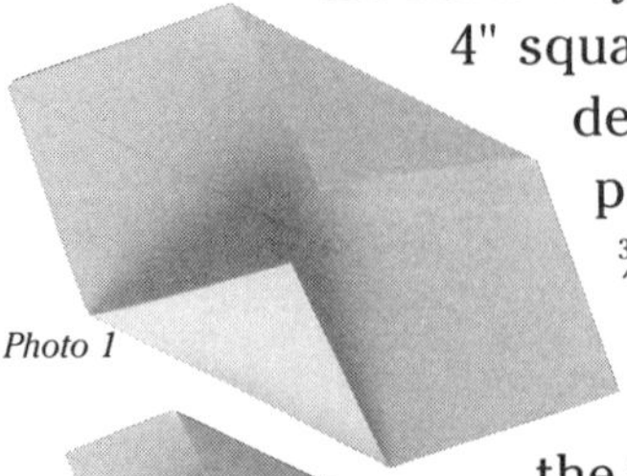

Photo 1

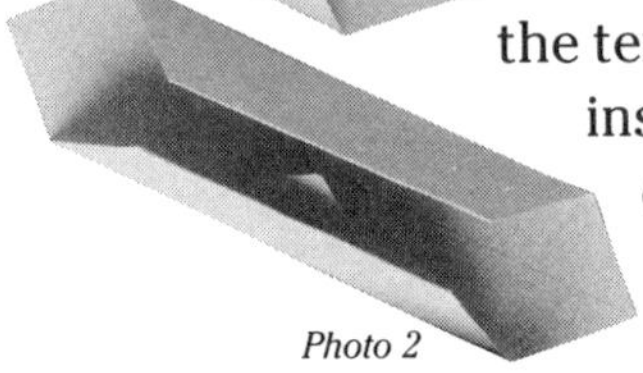

Cut the paper to size by using the templates. Draw a light line on the inside of the paper from corner to corner, and fold two opposing corners to the center line (see photo 1). Fold again to bring

Photo 2

Photo 3

the folded edge in figure 1 to the center line (see photo 2). Unfold and fold from the other two corners in the same manner (see photo 3). Unfold and cut as shown in photo 3. The dashed lines depict fold lines, and the solid lines depict cut lines.

Photo 4 shows how the flaps are folded to complete the box. Photo 5 shows the final box.

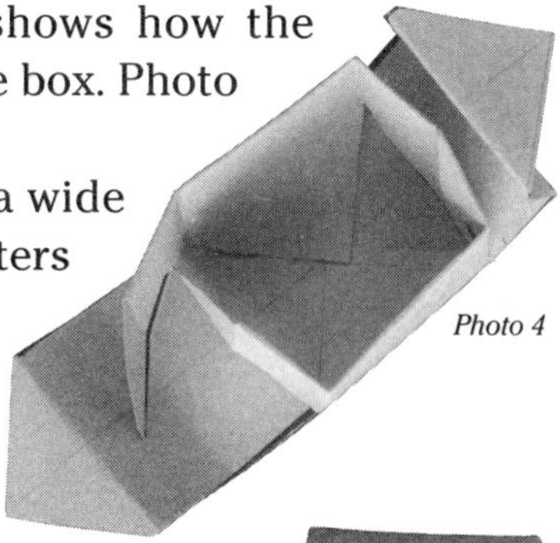

You can make boxes from a wide variety of material, and youngsters love using them for gifts, play, etc. I've even seen them used as coffins for pet insects and such. In December, my wife makes them as decorations for

Photo 4

our Christmas tree. My granddaughters love to make special boxes for their jewelry and personal keepsakes.

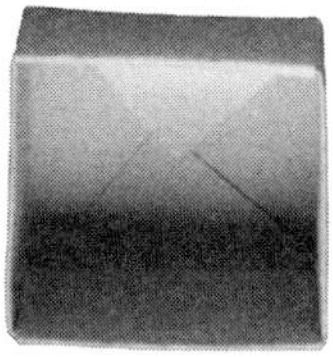

You can always make the box more durable by gluing all the sides together. Also,

Photo 5

you can cut out a square and place it in the bottom of the box to improve the appearance. Finally, encourage your grandchildren to draw and decorate their boxes to personalize them.

Lessons for Consideration:

- recycling
- thrift

Paddle
Wheel
Boat

Ages: 4-10

Materials Needed:

- a ½" x 3½" x 6" piece of pine. The end of a fruit box is a good source, though I usually use molding from the lumber yard.

- rubber bands

- a piece of flat plastic (easily obtained from a gallon milk jug)

- waterproof glue. (I use Elmer's Stix-All.)

- an empty thread spool (wood or plastic)

- four thumbtacks

Tools Required:

- scissors
- piece of wire bent into a hook
- ruler
- coping saw or narrow saw blade
- sabre saw (optional)
- pocketknife
- sandpaper

Safety Concerns:

Though this toy is quite harmless, building it involves tools that can injure. Be sure to give thorough safety lessons before you and your grandchildren use the sabre saw, scissors, or pocketknife.

Construction:

Using the sabre saw or pocketknife, cut the piece of wood into the shape shown in Photo 1. The dimensions are, of course, approximate. If you and your grandchildren want to taper the bow more to make the boat faster, feel free to do so. And if you want to make the well of the paddle wheel larger or smaller, go ahead. The thread spool you use will affect the size of the well, too.

Don't make the ⅜" pieces much thinner than those shown in photo 1. They must be fairly rigid to insure that they don't spring inward and bind the paddle wheel. After sawing the rough shape of the boat, smooth it and carve it for aesthetics. This is a great task for your grandchildren,

Photo 1

as they can fashion the boat until it suits them. They may want to paint it or carve their names into it, or they may decide that it looks fine as is. Whatever they decide will be fine.

Using the saw or saw blades, cut slits about ⅛" deep across the thread spool as shown in photo 2. Though only four slits are shown in the photo, the spool could have six or eight if you want. Be careful to keep the slit as narrow as possible so that the blade will wedge in tightly.

Push two thumbtacks into each end of the spool to anchor the rubber bands. Next, loop the rubber bands around the paddle supports. Using the bent wire hook, fish the rubber bands through the spool and over the thumbtack anchors.

For the "paddles," cut four pieces of flat plastic from a milk jug. The pieces should be as long as the spool and about ⅞" wide. Glue them into the slots of the spool and give the glue plenty of time to dry.

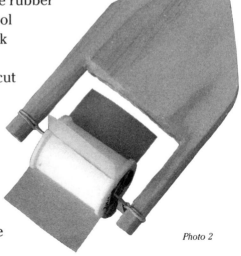

Photo 2

Now, wind up the paddle and try it out. If you wind it in one direction, the boat will go forward; wind it the other way and the boat goes backward. Of course, the tighter you wind the rubber band, the longer the boat will run. To make the boat go in circles, carve the bow so it's pointed toward one side.

Lessons for Consideration:

- thrift
- patience
- entertainment from everyday objects and situations

Willow Whistle

Ages: 10-15

Materials Needed:

- a short length of green willow twig (3" long by ⅜" diameter is ideal)

Tools Required:

- pocketknife

Safety Concerns:

Always give a knife safety lesson before opening a pocket-knife.

Construction:

First, you'll need to loosen the bark of the twig so the inner part can slip out. You can do this neatly with willow, but you'll need some patience. Lay the twig on its side on a smooth, firm surface. Using the handle of the knife, tap the bark along its length. Roll it slightly and tap it again until you've tapped the entire surface of the twig. Try to slip the bark off. You may need to do this tapping procedure a few times before the bark slips off cleanly.

Photo 1

Once you've finished tapping, carefully slip the bark off by pushing on the end of the wood interior plug while gripping the bark. If the bark is stubborn, peel ½" from the large end of the stick and put the peeled end in a vise. Grip the bark with your hand and twist and pull until it slips away. Be careful not to crush the bark tube as it slips free, since we'll use it later as the case for the whistle.

Another way to remove the bark is to use a 6" twig and peel the bark off half of it with a knife. This will give a 3" surface on the wood and a 3" surface on the bark. Thus you can grip both the wood and the bark and, by pulling in opposite directions, take the bark off as described above, after first tapping it. After slipping the bark off, remove the extra 3" piece of wood. (As youngsters, we seldom had access to a vise, especially if we were playing outdoors, so we often bit the free end of the twig while applying the wrenching motion. Parents will not recommend this maneuver— nor will I—especially if they have invested heavily in orthodontic improvements.)

Photo 1 shows a whole willow twig. Photo 2 shows the twig with the bark slipped off. Photo 3 shows the end-stopper plug and the shaved blowing-end plug separated from the whistle. (Note that the blowing-end plug is shaved to make one side flat. This allows air to be directed across the notched opening.) Photo 4 shows the two finished whistles.

Photo 2

bark

inner core

Note that there are different sizes of twigs shown; different sizes will make different sounds. Length is not critical either, except that the longer the twig, the harder it is to remove the bark.

Photo 3: end-stopper plug

blowing-end plug

To cut the notch, re-insert the inner core in the bark tube in the original position. Notch the bark and the inner core, which will provide support so that the bark tube doesn't collapse. The inner core can then be used for the blowing-end plug and the end-stopper plug.

After you cut a notch in the blowing end, insert the shaved plug there. Note that you should cut the notch so the square end is toward the blowing end of the whistle. (The whistle won't work if the notch faces the other way.) The plug for the opposite end must be adjusted by sliding it

blowing end

Photo 4

in and out to find the proper length. A little experimenting will soon make you an expert.

In the photo, you'll see that, at the blowing end of the whistle, the shaved plug directs a thin flow of air across the notch. This thin air stream vibrates the column of air in the

blowing end

hollow tube and causes the sound. When both the notch and the column of air in the tube are the right sizes, the whistle makes a loud and surprisingly clear and pleasant sound.

There's a lot of cutting and shaping in making this toy, so allow lots of time for it. It's a great item to make while you're on a lunch break during a day hike.

Like the straw tooter, you may find your grandchildren blowing on the whistle more than you'd like to hear. Remember, though, that they are learning and that these sounds, while perhaps annoying to you, are new and wonderful to them. Try to tolerate it longer than you think you can, then give them a lesson about respect for other people's peace and quiet.

Lessons for Consideration:

- simplicity
- elementary physics of sound and vibration

Bent Paper
Match Trick

Ages: 10-15

Materials Needed:

- paper match

Tools Required:

- pen or pencil

Safety Concerns:

Give a good fire safety lesson before using matches.

Construction:

This toy involves a humorous deception. Show a flat paper match to someone and allow him to inspect it thoroughly. Then make a mark on one side of the match. Wager which side of the match will show if the match is tossed in the air and allowed to fall on the floor. Just before you toss the match, suggest in an off-hand way that you should consider the "remote" chance that the match will land on its edge. The observer won't usually give that outcome much hope, so you can propose an outlandish bet to cover that possibility. Now you're ready to toss the match.

Hold the match between your first two fingers and your thumb, and use an underhand motion for the toss. As your hand sweeps upward, bend the match sharply in the middle —as close to 90-degrees as possible. Then release it and let it fall to the floor. A match bent in this manner will almost always land on its edge.

The observer will feel like he's been hoodwinked —which of course he has.

Nevertheless, youngsters delight in this kind of deception. They can master this simple trick in seconds, and they'll love trying it on their friends. A little practice will make them expert con artists.

Lessons for Consideration:

This simple trick can teach an invaluable life lesson: Never bet in another person's game. Here's a great opportunity to define the word "gullible" to your grandchildren and to teach them never to bet on a contest they don't understand. In addition, when they become the trickster, they will be able to lure their friends into ridiculous bets. So here's a good chance to teach them the importance of being chivalrous and letting your friends off the hook sometimes.

Cootie Catcher

Ages: 6-12

Materials Needed:

- square piece of paper (five, six, or eight inches)

Tools Required:

- pen or pencil

Safety Concerns:

None.

Construction:

I used a Cootie Catcher often when I was young. I made it in the classroom when the teacher wasn't watching and then used it at recess or lunchtime to tease others. Your younger grandchildren will have a lot of fun with it, and its construction is simple.

First, fold a sheet of paper diagonally so that the opposite corners meet. Fold the other corners the same way. This will locate the center of the sheet. Then, unfold the sheet and fold it again so that each corner is brought to

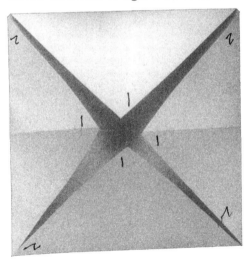

Photo 1

the center. (See photo 1; the original corners are marked "1".) When thus folded, new corners are formed (marked "2"). Fold the new corners to the opposite side, as in photo 2.

Next, form the shape until it looks like photo 3. It will help you to re-crease all the creases made previously. Unfold the flaps that have the "1" marked on them. This leaves a pocket in which you can insert your fingers to operate the Cootie Catcher.

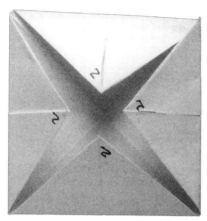
Photo 2

You can open the device in two directions. When you open it one way, draw some dots or faces on the inside. These will be the "cooties." When you open it the other way, leave the surface clean. You're now ready to catch "cooties."

Here's how we used to play with this toy: First, we'd let our friends see it opened to the clean surface, and we'd tell them it was a "cootie catcher." Then, we'd rub the device in their hair, close the clean surface, open the surface with dots showing, and gleefully exclaim that they had "cooties." Of course, we never really fooled anyone, but it was a silly means of teasing that provided a lot of fun. Sometimes, they had already seen the trick and would patiently allow us to try it on them. If we weren't dexterous enough to open the device properly, they would happily chide us for our clumsiness.

Youngsters will invent myriad uses for this simple item. One popular

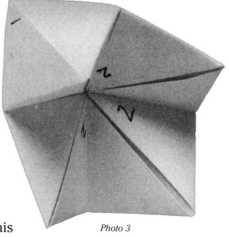
Photo 3

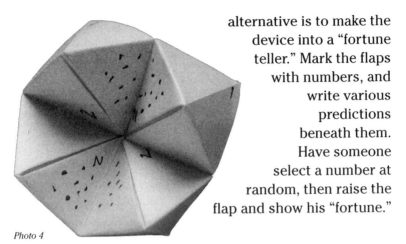

alternative is to make the device into a "fortune teller." Mark the flaps with numbers, and write various predictions beneath them. Have someone select a number at random, then raise the flap and show his "fortune."

Photo 4

Lessons for Consideration:

The most basic lesson you can teach with this device is thrift. For the cost of one piece of paper, your grandchildren and their friends can create hours of fun for themselves.

Photo credit: Nancy Pippin

Author Verne Steen with six of his eight grandchildren.
Left to right: Jennie, Brian, Clayton, Erin, Sean (sitting), and Alison.

About the Author

Verne Steen, a retired engineer, lives near Tucson, Arizona. His career included power plant design and construction in California and Washington, engineer and construction liaison on the Tokamak Fusion Test Reactor at Princeton University, resident field engineer at the Milford Geothermal Power Plant in Utah, and principal engineer for design for a satellite test facility at Kirkland Air Force Base in Albuquerque, NM.

He and his wife Shirley will soon celebrate their 50th wedding anniversary. They have three children and eight grandchildren.

More Great Books
from Mustang Publishing

The Complete Book of Golf Games
by Scott Johnston

Want to spice-up your next round of 18 holes? With over 80 great betting games, side wagers, and tournament formats, this book will delight any golfer. From descriptions of favorite games like Nassau and Skins to details on unusual contests like String and Bingo Bango Bongo, **The Complete Book of Golf Games** is essential for both casual hackers and the truly obsessed. **$9.95**

"A must acquisition . . . Entertaining as well as informative."
—Petersen's Golfing

The Complete Book of Beer Drinking Games
by Andy Griscom, Ben Rand & Scott Johnston

With over 500,000 copies sold, this book has become the imbiber's bible! From descriptions of classic beer games like Quarters and Blow Pong to hilarious new matches like Slush Fund and Beer Hunter—plus lots of funny cartoons, essays, and lists—this book remains the party essential. **$8.95**

"The 'Animal House' of literature." —Dallas Morning News

The Hangover Handbook
by Nic van Oudtshoorn

With 101 remedies for "humanity's oldest malady," this book is a godsend for imbibers who exceed their limits. Featuring descriptions of hangover cures from ancient to modern times, plus lots of funny drinking lore and trivia, **The Hangover Handbook** is a must in any well-stocked bar. **$6.95**

"The imbiber's bible for relief." —San Bernardino Sun

Europe for Free
by Brian Butler

If you're on a tight budget—or if you just love a bargain— this is the book for you! With descriptions of thousands of things to do and see for free all over Europe, you'll save lots of lira, francs, and pfennigs. **$9.95**

"Well-organized and packed with ideas." —Modern Maturity

Also in this series:

London for Free by Brian Butler $8.95

DC for Free by Brian Butler $8.95

Hawaii for Free by Frances Carter $8.95

The Southwest for Free by Mary Jane & Greg Edwards $8.95

Paris for Free (Or Extremely Cheap) by Mark Beffart $8.95

Northern Italy: A Taste of Trattoria
by Christina Baglivi

For the most delicious, most authentic, and least expensive meals in Italy, skip the *ristoranti* and head straight for *trattorie*, the small, unassuming cafes known only to locals. This guide, describing over 80 *trattorie* from Rome to Milan, is a must for the hungry traveler. **$12.95**

"Most valuable" —Tampa Tribune

Mustang books should be available at your local bookstore. If not, send a check or money order for the price of the book, plus $2.00 postage per book, to Mustang Publishing, P.O. Box 3004, Memphis, TN 38173 U.S.A. To order by credit card, call toll free 800-250-8713 (or 901-521-1406).

Allow three weeks for delivery. For rush, one-week delivery, add $2.00 to the total. *International orders:* Please pay in U.S. funds, and add $5.00 to the total for Air Mail.

For a complete catalog of Mustang books, send $1.00 and a stamped, self-addressed, business-size envelope to Catalog Request, Mustang Publishing, P.O. Box 3004, Memphis, TN 38173 U.S.A.